RICH IMAGINATION

More

Risqué Rhymes and Tantalising Tales

From

Richard Palmer

Warning
Contains adult and suggestive material.

First Printing 2017

ISBN   978-0-9525494-2-0

Published by
Anixe Publishing Ltd
London SE14 6QL
www.anixepublishing.co.uk
Cover Design by John Goodwin.

Ilustrations Public Domain Except
5 All Change At Crewe 47 Rumour Has It
& 52 Mixed Emotions all by Shutterstock

ACKNOWLEDGEMENTS

I would like to thank my wife Linda for sharing my life and frustrations in producing this book and my first book, 'Rich Inspirations' Promiscuous poems and Twisted tales. Without her help, understanding, patience and computer knowledge it would still be a pile of papers.

Thanks to the members of Paphos Writers Group for help, encouragement and feedback, each week for the past four years.

A special thanks to my friend and fellow writer John Goodwin of Anixe Publishing Ltd. for his help in publishing this book and his wife Jean for supplying endless cups of coffee.

Thanks to Dave Palmer (Fred) for encouragement and being my brother. Also my grandson Christopher Palmer for his technical support.

Thanks to friends Martin and Sally Walker, David and Carolyn Hart,

Peter Bruce and Carole Richards, Brian and Joan May and Mike and Rose Caldwell, plus many more who have endured my ramblings and given their views, often while enjoying a few cool drinks at Yialos Tavern, Coral Bay, Cyprus. Thanks to Pampos, Rena, George and Valentina, owners of Yialos and all the staff, for creating a wonderful setting, inspiring me to write many of the stories and poems

Richard Palmer

CONTENTS

1 ALL I NEED IS A HUG 2
2 SERVICE WITH A SMILE 4
3 I AM A POLITICIAN 6
4 WELL TACKLED 8
5 ALL CHANGE AT CREWE 10
6 YIALOS TAVERN BY THE SEA 13
7 THE POWER OF BELIEF...........................14
8 THE DAY THE EARTH STOOD STILL 16
9 MANCHESTER 18
10 THE GHOST OF MICKEY MOUSE 20
11 THE WONDER OF YOU 24
12 THE OPINIONATED WOMAN 28
13 SPIT AND POLISH 30
14 THE CALL GIRL..32
15 MY LITTLE SAT NAV 34
16 BONE OF CONTENTION 36
17 PAST HIS PRIME..38
18 A SPOT OF BOTHER 40
19 THE CHRISTENING....................................41
20 WHAT A LOAD OF TRIPE 45
21 WHAT A LOAD OF FROLICS....................46
22 SEX DRIVE 48
23 UP THE CREEK 50
24 MANHANDLED...52
25 ANTI-SOCIAL 54
26 TAKE IT LIKE A WOMAN..........................55
27 DEAR MR PRESIDENT...............................57
28 MY HERO...59
29 WHY ME...62
30 E BA GUM..64

31 GAZUMPED AND TRUMPED 65
32 FOR RICHER FOR POORER 66
33 A BUM DEAL 68
34 COUNTER MEASURES 71
35 SPEECHLESS 74
36 BREXIT 75
37 THE LEARNER DRIVER 77
38 THE SEMI SCOUSER...................................78
39 A POOR RELATIONSHIP 80
40 TOTALLY CONFUSED 82
41 CINDERELLA'S GHOST 84
42 LOVE HURTS 88
43 THE CONFESSION 92
44 AUTUMN 94
45 BEST MATES...96
46 THE POWER OF A SMILE 99
47 RUMOUR HAS IT.....................................100
48 BLIND DATE 102
49 THE GRASS IS ALWAYS GREENER. 104
50 FECKIN CORN 106
51 QUEST FOR LOVE,...................................109
52 MIXED EMOTIONS 113
53 THE WRITER'S DILEMMA 116
ABOUT THE AUTHOR................................119

RICH IMAGINATION

More

Risqué Rhymes and Tantalising Tales

From

Richard Palmer

An illustrated collection of poems and stories

1 ALL I NEED IS A HUG

All I need is a gentle hug
To pull on my heart strings, give them a tug
Show me I'm wanted, show me you care
hug me tight, fondle my hair
For you are the one that keeps me sane
You are the one that shares my pain
When I'm down and all alone
I know it's you I can phone
You're my rock, my best friend
I will love you to the end
We bond, we share

We love, we care
We've cried, we've laughed
We've been sad, we've been daft
We've argued, we've shouted
Our problems we've flouted
I was ill, you were there
My pain, you came to share
Your smile, your touch
Meant oh so much
I recovered, I felt well
But it was you who went through hell
Our feelings, our emotion
Show the world our true devotion
We've been together, we've been apart
Nothing changed from the start
The bond is strong, the love is true
That's why I need a hug from you
As we grow old so I'm told
Our bones will feel the cold
But together we'll fight this path
At adversity we will laugh
And at the end when our time arrives
We'll be happy we shared our lives
But right now, I need a hug
To pull on my heart strings, give them a tug
Show me I'm wanted, show me you care
Tell me you love me and forever be there.

2 SERVICE WITH A SMILE

This house is a mess, I have a hospital appointment and could be away for hours, said Andrew's wife Penelope, do you think you could do something about it before I get back,' Andrew, are you listening to me, I want the house sorting out'

Nag, nag, nag thought Andrew, she's always going on about something. The cleaner doesn't work properly, replied Andrew. 'Then service it, sort it or get a new one, you have always got an excuse. Penelope left for the hospital leaving Andrew in a disgruntled mood. I'm fed up of this life, he thought, do this, do that. Wouldn't mind if the time we spent together was pleasant, but it's not and as for a sex life, it's a joke, can't remember the last time, oh what's the use, I married her, just have to get on with it.

He continued with the newspaper daily crossword but his concentration was drawn to the nearly nude picture of a young pin-up girl on the adjacent page. Could do with some of that he mused, I may be fifty-seven but it doesn't stop me looking. He just stared at the picture and wondered how life would be with someone like that. Would clean the house all bloody day for her, ah what's the use and returned to the crossword. One down, six letter word for a sexy young girl, rub it in why don't you as he became agitated, bloody nympho!!

Better get this cleaner project sorted or she will be on my back for evermore. An hour later Andrew was whistling and singing his head off, all sorted he said to himself, life will be far better from now on, I just hope Penelope will be happier. A while later Penelope returned, she walked into the lounge to find Andrew naked, having

sex with an equally naked young girl who was bent over the
settee. 'What's going on, what are you doing screamed
Penelope and who is this young girl.' Andrew, full of new
found confidence replied, 'just doing what you asked dear,
the old cleaner was useless so I got this one and I am happy

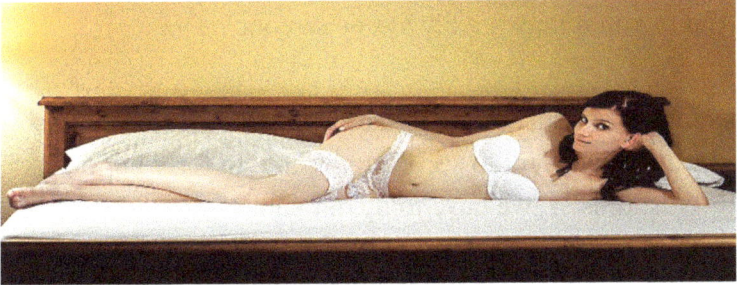

to service it every week.

3 I AM A POLITICIAN

I am a Politician, I say what I mean
But to you the public, I may not appear as I seem
It's a special language for the very exclusive
And to you it may not always be so conclusive

I studied it at university, it's designed to confuse the masses
The ones that went to secondary school in forty pupil classes
In Westminster, we have to up our game
With cameras on, people would think we are insane

We have to make decisions and oppose this and that
From some doddery old git who's deaf and blind as a bat
Shouldn't he retire, make room for someone younger
A fresh-faced lass, so the corrupt could easily bung her

We never answer no, we never answer yes
We just leave you confused, leave you to guess
The European parliament, now that's a another matter
Most are foreign and speak a different patter
But all around the world, when in parliament we sit
We know deep in our hearts, we talk a load of shit

4 WELL TACKLED

It had been a great night out on the town with his best mates celebrating his twenty second birthday. Many pubs and bars were visited resulting in a large consumption of alcohol. As the night continued, they met up with a group of girls out on a hen party and one particular young girl caught Jamie's attention. She looked stunning, really sexy with long dark hair, deep blue eyes and pouting lips. The little black lace dress showed off her fabulous figure, legs up to her armpits as the phrase goes with tantalising boob cleavage. Jamie was mesmerised and full of confidence fuelled by drink. The two groups merged together and he immediately got her up to dance, eager to be close and find out more about her. She was bubbly, although slightly intoxicated and warmed to Jamie's charm and good looks. Later, her friends decided to move on to another venue but she decided to stay with her new friend. With his mates now smashed drinking shots at the bar, Jamie suggested to his sexy friend that they take a taxi back to his flat, she incoherently agreed.

The heating was on, the lighting subdued, soft ballad music played from the television while candles flickered. A large glass of wine each completed the scene as she sank into the deep rich soft leather sofa, her legs slightly parted as her dress rose high showing a tantalising bit of black lace panties. Jamie sat close by, mouth and eyes wide open, he spoke to her but there was no response, she had passed out. He felt totally frustrated, his intoxicated brain was playing with his desires and high emotions. Should he carry on and go for it or leave her to sleep it off. It was a difficult decision as he gazed at her beautiful, peaceful body but his urges got the better of him and he decided to pursue his desires. His hand went under and round her slim waist feeling every inch, he moved the cushion allowing her body to lie more comfortable, feeling around her buttocks as he did so. She never stirred or made a murmur making it difficult for Jamie to decide what to do next. It was becoming urgent as time was passing by so he slid his hand under her parted legs, the soft flesh sending disturbing messages to his brain as his hand gently brushed against the soft lace panties. He became highly aroused and frustrated, he knelt in front of her, once again pushing his hands around her buttocks forcing his head down. His fingers found the vital thing he had been searching for, he thrust them forward, still she never moved, he went further and after a while he very slowly withdrew from her. He sat on the sofa, the tension oozing from his body, delighted that he had done it without her knowing. He smiled as the sports channel came on, happy that he could watch his

beloved rugby team play in the final now that he had managed to recover the remote control.

5 ALL CHANGE AT CREWE

Billy Jones was a young porter working for the railway company. He had been there for six years after leaving school and really enjoyed his job helping passengers with any questions or problems they may incur. For the past four years he had been courting Maisie a bubbly blonde but sometimes dizzy and scatter brained young lass who he totally adored. She worked in the railway cafe as a waitress and would pop round to see Billy during her break as they hated being apart. They had a very strong physical attraction towards each other which in the past had got them into a spot of bother.

One day, Billy was going about his platform duties amongst hundreds of passengers eagerly waiting for a train to take them on life's journey. Billy's break came and he entered the office, removed his jacket and tie then flopped onto an old red leather settee. Before he had time to shut his eyes, Maisie came bounding in full of energy and fiercely hugged him on the settee. Billy, although weary, was quickly aroused as her pouting lips sought his, her hands caressing his lean body. He responded quickly as his tongue searched her sensual mouth and his hands wandered over her torso feeling every inch of her sexual attributes. Things quickly got out of hand as clothing began to fall on the floor and very soon they were both totally naked, Maisie now bent over the office desk backwards, her hands stretched out behind her supporting her body, legs apart, while inviting Billy to make passionate love to her. The young virile lad did not need any encouragement, he burst into action and thrust himself into her, she howled with delight, her hands moving and straining to take the weight of Billy's writhing body. Suddenly, Billy grabbed hold of her and turned her round over the table, once again entering her with eager passion. Why have you changed position she said in a broken sentence as she shrieked and moaned as the love making reached fever pitch. Billy, now giving her all the energy he could muster said gasping, ' Everyone changes at Crewe.' A minute before climax Billy asked, 'Maisie, will you marry me '. There was no response apart from groans and shrieks, so he repeated the request. Just then the station master walked in on the scene and shouted Maisie, there are nearly a thousand people on the platform refusing to get on the train until you say yes, so, will you marry him'. Billy, now totally delirious in passion gave one final surge and Maisie screamed, yes, yes, yes oh bloody yes.' Thank you said the station master, you can take your hand off the Tannoy switch now '.

6 YIALOS TAVERN BY THE SEA

In the back of beyond alongside the sea
Is a Cypriot tavern, so full of charm
The foaming white waves, there for all to see
And an atmosphere of peace and total calm
The Cypriot owners so genuine and caring
Tending to your every need
Cypriot cuisine cooked for sharing
Ensuring you have a top-class feed
A special cocktail, a secret recipe
For you to sip and savour the taste
Made with love and care for you and me
To be enjoyed, but not in haste
Refreshing cold beer in the heat of the sun
No sign of a cloud in the sky
A luxury yacht, people having fun
As very slowly it passes by
We dream and wish of paradise
And think, 'are we jealous'
I'm sure it must be very nice
But to me paradise is Yialos

7 THE POWER OF BELIEF

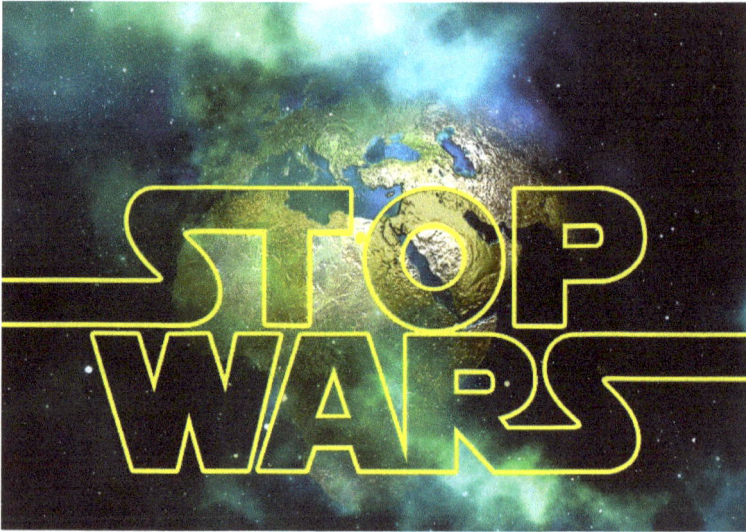

What is the story of Christmas, does anybody know
It used to be about Mary and Joseph and a baby who had a glow
His name was Jesus and he was born in a stable
Three wise men brought him presents to be used when he was able
The son of God they said he was, a disciple of all that was good
He performed miracles and preached the gospel from where he stood
But not all the people believed in the world he taught
And fighting broke out so a demand for his arrest was sought
What is the story of Easter, does anybody know
It used to be about Jesus, once a baby with a glow
He was nailed to a cross, a sight of total despair
And put on show to warn others not to go there

Crucified and in pain, he was buried but then unfurled
And went on to preach Christianity throughout the world
But where is he today in a world of total distrust
Where cities like Aleppo are being turned into dust
Afghanistan, Libya, Iraq, where millions have died
Surely, he could have stopped it if he tried
Belief is a power, so great in the mind
And Christianity is just one religion of many a kind
Jesus was special, someone to adore
But in this modern world, he cannot stop a war.

8 THE DAY THE EARTH STOOD STILL

The sun never rose that morning
The birds never gave a tweet
At first, I thought I was dreaming
But then I pulled off the flannelette sheet
The clouds were grey and overcast
No breeze would move them at all
I stared at the glorious fir trees
Standing rigid and ever so tall.
Movement of life had diminished
To a point of being extinct
As I gazed with wide open eyes
Fearful that I blinked.
Had the Earth suddenly stood still
Was I dreaming, was I ill
How long for, a year, a month a day
Was this it, would things always be this way.
No morning sunrise, no chorus at dawn
No evening sunset, no golden corn

A moon lost forever in a warp of time
No twinkling stars in an atmosphere of decline.
Three days went by in this place of gloom
As I tried to sleep in my eerie room
But in the morning the sun rose high
And I asked the question, why, oh why.
A voice in my head made me twitch and nod
It was a calling from heaven, the voice of god
I'm sorry my son for the doom and gloom
But things will be normal very soon.
It was my birthday, I went out for the night
And I turned off the switch that gave you light
Three days went by, I was totally gone
But the good news my son, I switched you back on!

9 MANCHESTER

This is our city, this is our home
A place of freedom, a place to roam
A bond of friendship lies at our feet
As we talk to strangers when we meet
A city of culture, a city of fame
Buildings and rock bands, too many to name
Diverse in all aspects, a city so proud
As we mingle in concerts with a mixed-race crowd
Defiant against evil, only love we share
As we live our lives, but some in despair
Blown up by cowards, sick in the mind
Alien to us, not our kind
But life goes on and united we stand
As we listen to music from our favourite band
Defiant in manner, bonded so strong
To send out a message to those in the wrong
We will not be broken, we do not scare
As for your existence we do not care
You are sick and evil beyond our mind
This city does not want you or your kind
So hug another, say I am your friend
And hope one day, this misery will end
In the meantime, be happy with laughter
Look forward to life now and hereafter
Remember the loved ones blown up by a bomb
No concerts for them, their life has gone
No sense no reason, just something rotten
But Manchester will make sure they are never forgotten.

In Memory of Those Who Lost Their Lives.

10 THE GHOST OF MICKEY MOUSE

Good morning girls, I have some exciting news for you, said Kate and Millie's mother, Angela. Your father and I are thinking of taking you to Disneyland in Florida for two weeks during school holidays, what do you think?

At aged eleven and twelve this was a schoolgirl's dream and they shouted 'Yes, Yes, Yes, oh yes please and became very excited. They had never been to another country before, only to Cornwall and a week camping in Scotland. They set off for school and could not wait to tell all there friends their good news. I knew as their mother what the reaction would be and I also felt their excitement. I booked the holiday, we would be staying in a five-star hotel close to the theme park so the girls could go every day if they wished.

School finished a few days later and I took the girls into town shopping for new clothes and other items they would require. At times in crowded shops, I had to tell the girls to calm down as their enthusiasm was overwhelming and rather noisy. New suitcases completed the shop and the girls eagerly went home to pack. A few days later, amid cloud and drizzle, we took off from Manchester airport.

We arrived at the luxury hotel in brilliant sunshine and having unpacked, set about exploring the area. The following day we entered Disneyland, the look on the girls' faces was something to be cherished forever so I took some photographs while they were otherwise engaged. There were cartoon characters everywhere, but the girls had their sights set on a large ice cream each. They ran off to the ice cream parlour to choose their favourite flavour. Just then a Disney float with Mickey Mouse waving to everyone, passed by obscuring our view of the girls and as it moved on we realised that the girls were no longer at the stall. Panic set in, the place was heaving with people. Kevin my husband checked with the ice cream seller but he had been so busy he never noticed in which direction the girls went. He tried to find them in the immediate location but it was hopeless as the crowds pushed passed him. We informed security and their names were announced over the tannoy time and time again but there was no response. I was in tears but all we could do was search along with security.

Eventually I would find out about their amazing adventure.

They had wandered into a building through a back door where a show was going on but ended up in the basement. Along a disused corridor, they found an old cobweb covered lift that looked as though it had not been used for years, the lights did not work and it was difficult to see. They pressed the buttons and to their amazement the doors opened. Being so young, they thought it was a great adventure so they stepped inside in total darkness and pressed a button. The lift began to creak, they held each others hand wondering if they had done the right thing but it was too late, with a few creaks and groans the lift slowly began to move. Down and down it went, they could here the grinding of the mechanism, it seemed to be never ending. Eventually it came to a halt and the silence was scary. They tried frantically to press the buttons for it to go up again but in the darkness the doors suddenly opened. They pushed back against the lift wall, not knowing what to expect. Lights shone in their eyes, music could be heard with lots of laughter, giving a feeling of happiness. Their inquisitive minds urged them to step out of the lift with much anxiety, they did so very slowly. After a while their eyes adjusted to the new-found surroundings, mouths opened in pure amazement as there before them was a mini theme amusement park stuck in a time warp. An elderly creature slowly shuffled towards them with the help of a walking frame, a female of similar age by his side. 'Hello' he said, welcome to our theme park, my name is Mickey Mouse and this is my partner Minnie. As you could imagine, the girls were in complete shock and almost disbelief but they were soon convinced as more characters arrived. Let me introduce you to my nieces Millie and Melody and this is my older sister Amelia and her sons Morty and Ferdie. Just then more characters arrived to see what all the commotion was about. 'Hello, I am Donald Duck said the elder and this is my partner Daisy and these are my nephews Huey, Dewey and Louie. Mickey said, 'Come in, let us show you round.' Just then an old dog was struggling to jump up at Mickey but his arthritic legs refused to let him do so. 'This is Pluto my dog and this is Goofy.' The theme park was brightly lit with many attractions and in full working order. The girls spent a fabulous afternoon with their new-found friends, it was without doubt the best day of their lives.

On eventually finding my daughters, I felt a great feeling of relief but could not help myself from scolding them for wandering off and causing us so much worry and anxiety. 'Where have you been,' I shouted, 'we have been worried sick and you have missed all the Disney cartoon characters all afternoon. '

My daughters replied, 'REALLY?'

11 THE WONDER OF YOU

Born in a small English country village, miles from the nearest town, Sam Jones, grew up with little knowledge of the outside world. His parents ran a small farm and even at the age of eighteen, Sam had rarely travelled any further than the local market where his father would sell produce to pay for their meagre existence. Due to falling out of a barn onto farm machinery when he was a small boy, Sam required major surgery which included damage to his brain. As a result, he missed much of his early school life and the little knowledge he had was gained from working on the farm. As time passed, Sam became restless and felt it was time he began to explore, not just Britain, but other countries. Due to his injuries and circumstances and the fact that he was slow in speech and lacked education, Sam had become the butt of jokes and regarded by some as the village idiot. He was a bit of a dreamer and fantasized about becoming an international statesman or prime minister or president of a major country. A position where he could change the world for the better. There was no end to his fantasies but there was also virtually no hope of it happening.

A year or so later, Sam received substantial compensation and after taking care of his parents, decided to go somewhere exciting. He chose the bright lights of Las Vegas, the total opposite of his present life.

He arrived at the height of the season and was totally mesmerised by all the hustle and bustle plus the thousands of lights. He wandered round the arcades, went to shows and learnt to play blackjack in the casinos. He felt a bit ordinary as he walked amongst the punters, the ladies in their beautiful evening dresses and men in dinner jackets and bow tie. The following day he found an almost new white dinner jacket for sale and bought it. A local store supplied a new white frilled shirt and bow tie and Sam was transformed and put into a world he had never known before. That night he played blackjack with the air and grace and confidence of James Bond, plus he won some money. He left the casino and walked into a show bar where people could get up and sing on stage. Sam did not have much of a voice, any warbling was done in the fields away from all except the birds and the bees plus the animals he was attending to who never complained about the racket he was making. After choosing a table, he put his hand up to raise the attention of the waiter who seemed to ignore him in the busy atmosphere. Before he had chance to lower his arm, he was grabbed by two burly men and hauled up on the stage. He was unaware that the compare had just asked for someone to come up and sing. Panic set in as he was placed in front of the mike, the music began to play as the words came up on a screen. It was Sam's favourite song and he sang his heart out except this time it wasn't the birds and the bees, it was a thousand people. At the end, Sam failed to understand what was happening, there was the entire audience on their feet applauding, whistling, screaming for more. The compare reacted quickly and set Sam up to do another song, then another, they could not get enough of him. He stood there in his dinner jacket somewhat confused but elated at the response. He returned to his table and as he took his jacket off he found a note in the lining. It read, to whom it may concern, this is a magical jacket and whoever owns it will take on all the attributes, habits and talents of the person who last wore it. Take care of it and only give it to someone worthy who will live up to your expectations. Sam sat there dazed and confused trying to understand the meaning when suddenly it dawned on him that the reason for his success tonight was the jacket, but that was crazy. He also realised that the previous owner was a great singer and entertainer, but who!

Sam returned to his hotel room, totally bewildered by the events of the night. He took off the dinner jacket, poured a drink and just sat there staring at the garment. He stood up and slowly paced round the room then burst into song, it was rubbish, out of tune, could not hit the high notes. He new what he had to do next but the thought of what might happen scared him, right now he was back to being Sam, the lad they called the village idiot. After half an hour and a couple of strong brandies, he put on the jacket and immediately felt stimulated. He warily began to sing, the song flowed beautifully, he recorded himself on his phone so he could play it back and listen, ensuring himself that this was really happening.

The following morning Sam woke to the sound of the phone ringing, it was Tim Burrows a local entertainment agent and manager who had been in the audience the previous night. 'I'd like to meet up and discuss your singing career,' said Tim. But I can't, Sam cut short, 'when' he asked. How about this afternoon in your hotel lounge,' said Tim, 'say three pm'? Sam realised that he had almost given the game away, 'that's fine' said Sam, 'see you later.'

The meeting went fairly smoothly although Sam was a bit bewildered by it all. The so-called village idiot had just been offered a fantastic deal to sing at the main venues in Las Vegas and if successful, a recording contract for a single and an album. This is mad, he thought and he knew that if he was not wearing the dinner jacket on the night, none of it was possible. Tim wanted him to wear a red jacket but Sam was having none of it and told him the white one was his lucky charm. Tim agreed and a contract was signed.

Several months later, Sam, who by now was a household name having hit the number one spot in the country and abroad and playing to packed venues most nights, was invited to sit at the table with the President at a grand charity ball. As the night went on and the drink flowed, Sam excused himself to make a visit to the gents' cloakroom. The President also decided to go and both removed their jackets, hanging them up. Sam, having used the ablutions, picked up the jacket but due to the warm night, carried it and placed it over the back of his chair. The President returned to the table wearing his jacket but appeared to be uneasy and acting in a strange manner. By the end of the night all his protocol had disappeared and he was babbling away like a village idiot. Due to recent events since his election, no one at the table noticed any difference.

12 THE OPINIONATED WOMAN

Stop screaming! it's only a man
I don't care, I don't give a damn
What use are they, what are they for?
I don't use them anymore.
They're just trouble and strife
All they want is a working wife
To cook, clean and make things tidy
Then off to the pub every Friday
Pissed with their mates
Falling over garden gates
Make love to me they slobber
As they sway and hover
Not a pretty sight
As they grope and groan through the night
Bad breath and stubble
They're nothing but trouble
So, what do you do for sex
When you need a kiss, a couple of pecks
You may think I am totally mad
But I get the same effect from a Brillo pad
It's rough and ready and very coarse
But not quite up for intercourse
And when it's wet, it lies there limp
But doesn't moan like a wimp
And if I want sex a little later
I'll use my friend, the vibrator.

13 SPIT AND POLISH

The instructions on the packet were very clear
But the cost of it was far too dear
To dye my hair is what I required
For this old and grey look was very tired
Put a spark into my life, surprise my friends
Dye it black, repair split ends
Some new clothes, a whole new style
Look years younger for a while
Every six weeks, another dye
The cost was way far too high
Boot polish, that's the answer
It will make a fine enhancer
Ten tins I bought, should last a while
As on my hair I began to pile
Jet black in minutes, oh so cool
The girls will love it, they'll totally drool
Out on a date I need to impress
As I meet a stunner in her new dress
In virgin white she looked a dream
We got on well, she seemed so keen
I'll walk you home if that's alright
As we stepped out into a stormy night
Suddenly it began to rain
And I realised this could be a pain
She asked me for a tender kiss
An opportunity I could not miss
I held her close and stroked her hair
But to stare at her dress I did not dare
A big black mark did appear
As the rain ran past my ear

The boot polish was running over her dress
In a very short time she looked a mess
I said, is there any chance of another date
She replied, for you I think it's a little late
I stood there feeling in total despair
And wished I had never dyed my old grey hair.

14 THE CALL GIRL

Darling, answer the phone, I'm washing my hair
Not now dear, I'm fixing a light standing on a chair
Could be important like a family matter
Could be a cold call with sales patter
If it's important they will ring again
If it's a sales call they're just a pain
An hour later the phone again rang
Darling, this wallpaper I'm about to hang
I can't answer, I'm on the loo
Any suggestions what to do
Check the number when we are free
And find out who it could be
Maybe auntie Mary in hospital has died
If so we should be there by her side
Could be uncle Bill with his heart attack
We never keep in touch, never keep track
The numbers dead, there's no telling who
I am really worried, what should we do

Ring the hospital or auntie Flo at the farm
No don't do that, it will just cause alarm
Again it rang, with my knickers twisted, I hopped
Just to get there as it stopped
Nerves now frayed, blood pressure high
What can it be I stressfully cry
It rings again, to my ear it did fly
'Hello my dear, can I interest you in P.P.I

15 MY LITTLE SAT NAV

I have a little sat nav, it whispers words to me
Turn left in 200 metres, there's a junction there you see
I thank her for her courteous manner then turn into a lane
'Recalculating' she calmly says I think, *what a bloody pain*

In 300 metres please turn right and continue for a mile
She is so nice and pleasant, you can't help but give a smile
I manoeuvre to the right and continue down the lane
Then in a gentle voice she says 'recalculating' again

Now this little lane is one car wide, high hedges either side
When suddenly, in front of me is a river with flowing tide
Now I'm a patient person so I wait for her calming voice
Make a U-turn she tells me but that is not a choice

There's no room to do that and forward is out of bounds
My patience wearing thin this satnav cost many pounds
Make a 'U' turn she repeats in a tone now changed pitch
Sod off, sod off' I scream and shout, you stupid feckin bitch

She suddenly goes silent, I'm left struggling on my own
In the middle of nowhere and without my bloody phone
'Where've you gone you stupid bitch, I begin to lose my rag
'Hormones playing up again, you horrible, disgusting slag

Still no sound she's gone to ground,
I change her for a bloke
He says reverse, I give a curse
for this is no laughing joke

But after a mile, I begin to smile
as I face the right direction
Then she buts in, says where've you bin,
you need to make a correction

I've had enough, the days been tough
so I begin to sing
But all I can hear from my sat nav here
 is the bitch saying RECALCULATING.

16 BONE OF CONTENTION

Every bone in my body aches a bit more each day
I've tried taking pills and medicine but the pains won't go
away
It's as you get older so I'm told
And the weather affects it, especially when it's cold.
Stiff in the morning as I try to unwind
But unable to find relief of any kind.
An Osteopath, could that be the answer
To return me to being a top-class dancer.
I realise those days are no more
Now all I ask for is a permanent cure
A specialist I need before it's too late
Someone to cure the daily grate
But that costs money, too much for me
So, I'll have to suffer with my dodgy knee
The National Health, but could I wait
It takes forever to get a date

The operation done, I'll be fine
But in the meantime, I'm in decline
How long for an op? I asked the staff
An op, an op, you 'avin a laugh
Government cuts, that's all we get
So, an early op you can forget
We're skeleton staff, we can do no more
So please, we're busy, there's the door.

17 PAST HIS PRIME

At ninety-five, Fred was barely alive and his wife was much the same
He did nowt because of gout and his wife was really lame
He fancied some thrills, took some pills and gave the wife one or two
The effect could be stunning, the plan cunning, she said, 'do you know what to do'
'I'll try to remember how to use my member, but it's been a long, long time
She said, climb on here, Fred my dear, everything will be fine
He tried to move to get in the groove but his body wouldn't respond
He said, I think ma dear we're past the year of a natural sexual bond
Let's watch T.V, wait and see if the pills are any good
Cos ma dear, I seriously fear, I am no longer a super stud
Fred was right, they waited all night, but nothing did occur
So, he took some more, just to make sure, but didn't get a stir
His wife said, your members dead and so I think maybe
We should forget the idea, for I fear, we are too old to have a baby.

18 A SPOT OF BOTHER

It's just a little pimple, it sits upon my nose
I wish I could remove it or have it on my toes
It's there every morning, right before my eyes
Bright red and ugly, it just lies and lies
I've tried to squeeze it tightly, burst it I cannot
The skin is hard as nails, it will never rot
So, what's a man to do, especially on a date
She said, 'I'll pick a spot' so please don't be late
I covered it in cream and thought, 'do I really care'
Forget about the pimple, forget it's even there
But when I met my date, she simply said, 'hello'
Took one look at me and said, 'I have to go'
Is there something wrong? something you want to share
She said, 'you're not bad looking,' but you haven't got any
hair
You could always wear a wig, so a cure is quite simple
But you haven't got a hope of me, going out with that
pimple.

19 THE CHRISTENING

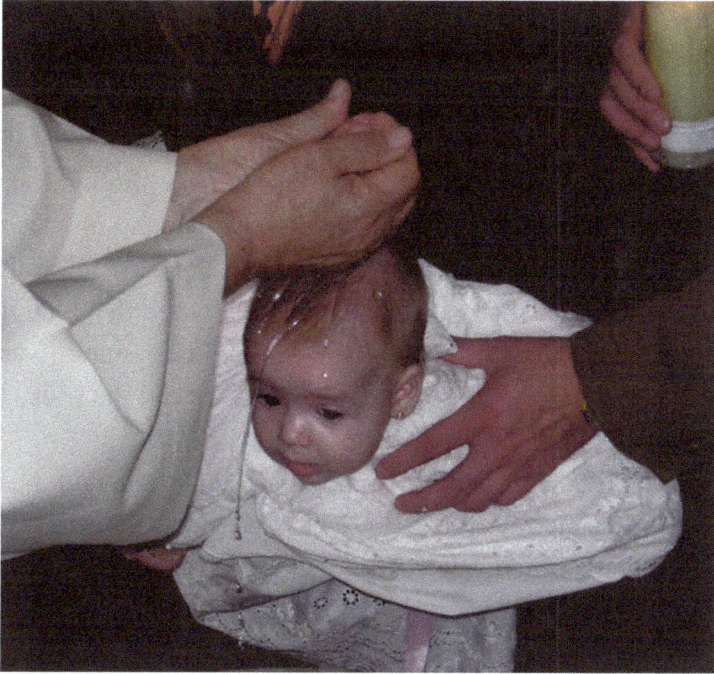

During the early part of my existence, I lived in a warm cosy home but there was no light. It was also small with very little room to move. At times there were loud rumblings and it felt as though everything around me was going to collapse. As time passed, my home was extended and I was able to move around a bit more. There was a constant banging noise which was a bit annoying but very little I could do about it. I was not in a good position to move so it was a case of wait and see what happens.

Eventually due to circumstances beyond my control, I was bodily dragged out of my home. I put up a good fight, there was lots of blood and yelling but to no avail, I was forced out. Severely traumatised, I cried for a long time, my warm cosy home was no more.

As time passed I became mentally and physically stronger and moved in with my parents We always had lots of visitors, especially at weekends when the relatives would come round with presents and make a fuss of me. One day this old auntie came and was twittering away through her false teeth, spluttering all over the place. I thought, how can I get rid of her without being rude. Did not have to wait long. As she drew her face close to mine, I farted that loud it almost blew her hat across the room. The smell was diabolical and she was so embarrassed but it did the trick, I never saw her for months.

I went out with my parents a lot, train and bus journeys but mainly in the car. There were lots of walks to the local park which was very nice. I used to watch the birds flying overhead and settling in the trees as the clouds gently passed by.

One day all my relatives came to the house and there was lots of chatter and fussing about. Eventually they left along with my parents and me. We travelled some distance in the car and came to a large building. It was very impressive and I was surprised to see all my family there. They all sat down in rows of seats, I was ushered to the front. There was music playing and lots of bright lights everywhere. Suddenly all my rellies started singing, or they thought they were singing, sounded more like fifty tom cats on heat out on the tiles.

I was swiftly bodily lifted up, a large nicotine stained hand went round my neck, I panicked, then panicked even more as the other hand went between my legs and grasped my bum. I thought, bloody pervert and stared into his eyes with a grim look of disgust. I must have had a dirty face as he began to wash it, then without warning he tried to drown me in a large tub of water. My life flashed before me, I thought, this is the end. With a bit of warning I could have held my breath but I had just exhaled and farted at the same time. He brought me up spluttering all over the place, I looked at my mum who could see my concern, she said, 'don't worry darling, the vicar has just christened you.'

20 WHAT A LOAD OF TRIPE

Left on my own, wife gone away
nothing to eat during the day
Can't boil an egg or make anything on toast
Can't make an omelette or Sunday roast
Off to the shop for a package meal
Nice roast beef or a piece of veal
Can't read the label, eyes a blur
To bring my glasses, it didn't occur
I ask an old dear, 'can you read that'
'Sorry son, I'm as blind as a bat'
I squint and peer at the label
Then ask the assistant whose name is Mabel
But she just walks on, doesn't care a jot
If I can read or I cannot.
In total frustration I grab a packet or two
And rush off home to make a beef stew
I heat it up and put it on a plate
And think to myself, this will be great
But it was absolutely foul, a load of tripe
And with a napkin, my face I wipe
You couldn't eat it, there were no flavours
Oh stuff it all, I'm off to Specsavers.

21 WHAT A LOAD OF FROLICS

Going home from school I saw a little lamb
It was frolicking in a field close to it's mam
I watched as it jumped three foot in the air
Then landed on a rock, it's leg in dire repair
I leapt into the field and held the little lamb
Feeling very guilty as I took it from it's mam
I nursed it back to health, it meant the world to me
It sat upon my lap as we watched the evening T.V
One day it followed me all the way to school
I had to bring it back, apparently there was a rule
I cried and cried for hours, it was awful being apart
I should never have rescued it from the very start
The feelings and emotions were far too much too bear
And I got to a stage where I didn't really care
But I loved my little lamb while he was alive
But I love him even more on gas marked number five
He lies by the potatoes next to the peas
Covered in rich gravy, I can eat him with ease
There are no mixed emotions it was just a matter of course
Before I served him up with lashings of mint sauce.

22 SEX DRIVE

At thirty-six years old life was fabulous for Paul Watson. He had a high-flying job as a stockbroker in the city, which he loved, was very highly paid, owned a lovely property in the countryside, drove a new range rover and had a beautiful, young sexy wife. There were no children which allowed his wife Dawn to work full time in her own business as a beautician. They had been married for five years and enjoyed a wonderful loving sex life.

Dawn was in the process of moving to a larger shop in the city and there was a great deal to sort out. Eventually she moved in and business rapidly began to expand as time passed. She took on more staff to cope with the increasing clientele and found herself working late most evenings. As the months passed by, Paul noticed that his wife was becoming less interested in their sex life and put it down to the pressure of work. She would arrive home around seven thirty each evening looking agitated and exhausted and after a meal, would retire to bed early. Paul often took the opportunity of an early night and cuddled up for some sexual activity but each time over a month or so Dawn pushed him away. Paul was not a happy man.

One day, Dawn had to take her car and leave it at the garage for a service, so Paul followed and dropped her off at work. She received a phone call to say that the car would not be ready until the following day so Paul picked her up in the evening. They entered a built-up area with thirty miles per hour speed limit which dropped to twenty miles per hour outside a hospital. Suddenly Dawn lay back in her seat and became very agitated and excited, her short skirt showing off her well-developed legs which had now parted as she

stretched out. She had a smile on her face and began to shake with her hands rubbing her thighs. Paul thought she was having an epileptic fit and pulled the car into a side road. Dawn, Dawn, he shouted in a distressed voice, what's the matter, do you want to go to hospital? That was fabulous, she exclaimed. What was fabulous, enquired Paul with a deluded look. She just lay there silent and smiling, then after a few minutes she sighed and said, 'one makes me tingle, two makes me excited, three finishes me off altogether and the vibration from four road rumble strips is more than most women can cope with.' ' Do you come home this way every day' asked Paul. ' Yes,' Dawn replied. Paul smiled, realising he had found the solution to his troubled   sex
life.

23 UP THE CREEK

At 7.0.am I was walking along the beach looking out over the estuary. It had been a severely wild night with gale force winds, thunder and lightning plus torrential rain. Sleep had been difficult and I hoped the early morning stroll would clear my head.

Suddenly I was there looking down at her, she looked seriously rough lying in the sand face down, partly on her side. An old sunbed was lying on top of her and she was covered in sand and in much distress. Eventually I managed to drag her off the beach, I took her home and cared for her and gave her a new life. It took a long time and we became very close.

Later when she reached peak condition, I took her on holiday and stayed in a hotel overlooking the sea. I lovingly stared at her as she lay stretched out on the beach, she looked amazing. I slowly managed to get her in the water, it was difficult to know how she would manage it after the past experience.

I sat on top of her, jerking myself back and forth, I heard a groan as I increased my pace. You could hear the grinding as my buttocks and thighs were exerted to their limits. My hands and arms vigorously pulling her towards me then releasing as we both surged forward. This was pure ecstasy, our bodies vibrating in perpetual motion. Time passed, I was exhausted but I felt she could go on and on. She took everything I gave her there was no let up, then suddenly, as my torso pushed hard into her, I pulled my head and arms backwards. Due to sheer force, both rowlocks broke, I fell backwards and the oars floated off into the sea leaving me "Up the creek," without a paddle.

24 MANHANDLED

I woke up that morning feeling very amorous and excited, as later I was to meet a new friend who I had found on the internet. Even though we had never met, I had managed to obtain enough information to determine that we were meant for each other. She was colourful, bright, graceful and had all the charm and character a man could desire.

I had preferred younger models in the past, there was a vibrant feeling about them when you first got together, but after a while they lacked charisma and would often let you down. You paid them a lot of attention and pampered to their needs. You loved them with care and affection but very often you got nothing back in return, they just failed to respond. I became very disillusioned, hence my time spent looking for a more mature friend with greater values.

We met, I was just speechless and just stood and stared. She was everything I had ever dreamed of in life, pure class and absolutely beautiful. I slowly moved forward and embraced her, my heart pounding with exhilaration. She did not move, just stood there looking stunning. I ran my hands over her exquisite body and apart from a tight-fitting strap, I slowly removed her top. There was still no movement so I caressed all her features, yes, I thought, I could certainly be in love with you for the rest of my life. I reached down below and found the vital spot, I exposed my tool and slowly inserted it inside her, pulling on it hard to let her know it had gone all the way. A couple more jerks and she went wild, I was ecstatic then as the juices began to flow, she purred like a kitten.

I put the starting handle back in the boot, put her into first gear and roared off into the countryside.

25 ANTI-SOCIAL

I'm only one of many, just a little ant
I work hard all day and never puff and pant
I don't ask for pay and never claim the dole
I share a house with friends, we built it in a hole
We never whinge and moan, we never go on strike
We haven't got a union, we told them to take a hike
We never hurt each other, there's only time for love
And our religion, does not come from above
There is no need for wealth, all we want is food
To sustain our busy lives and bring up the family brood
There is no central heating, carpets or hot water
No financial strain for a son or a daughter
We don't cause bother or ever make a fuss
So why, oh why, do humans stamp on us
Should we stand and fight, bite them where it hurts
Crawl up men's trousers, explore ladies' skirts
But unlike humans our natures are very pure
All we want is peace, not a drawn-out war
So next time you're out and you see a little ant
Walk the other way and forget the rave
and rant.

26 TAKE IT LIKE A WOMAN

A new discovery, they said it would be great
For all those young people who panic when their late
 Unprotected sex was something totally new
And it gave the young people a different point of view
No need to carry condoms in a packet of three
Just take a little pill after you've had your tea
No need to worry if he doesn't pull out
Just enjoy the moment and shout and shout and shout
The baby boom began, it was totally bliss
As all the courting couples gave each other a kiss
But some had sex with anyone, anyone at hand
And they became well known for a quick one-night stand
Sex every night, they couldn't keep still
Then one day in their life, they forget to take the pill
I'm pregnant! they scream, I'll take an after pill
But sadly, it had not been discovered so pregnant you are still
He should have worn a condom, not rely on these
But you can't trust a bloke, when he's got you naked on your knees.
Party time is over, I'm now a mother of two
If the pill had not been discovered, I 'd put the blame on you
But I will just have to get on with all that I have got
For it's not really a man's fault, it's just that I forgot.

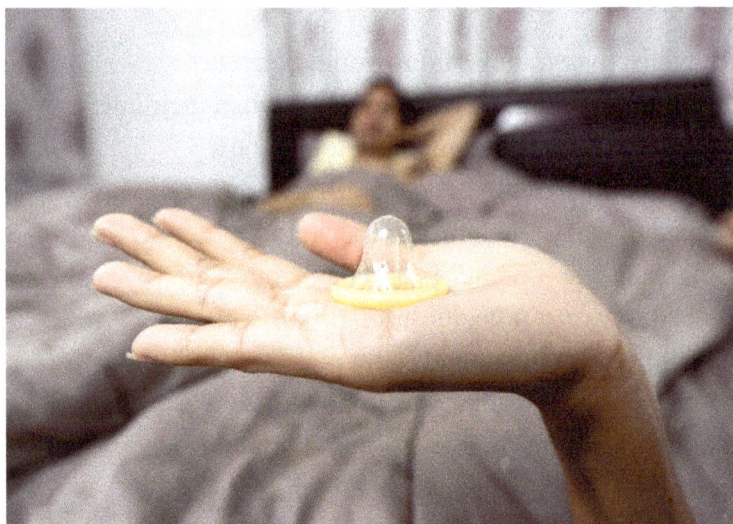

27 DEAR MR PRESIDENT

Dear Mr President.

First, let me congratulate you on conning and deceiving all your fellow Americans who you managed to brainwash and convince that you were the ideal candidate for the presidential elect. I congratulate you even more for being able to stand in front of millions of people around the world and give out false promises until it went dark each day for months. As a result, you are now the President of the United States of America.

It has come to my ears that you intend to do some crazy things, not normally a problem to a short arsed Mexican peasant like me, you are the president, you can do what you like. However, I do have serious concerns about a rumour going round that you intend building a wall round Mexico to stop greasy money and job grabbing little bastards like me, (your words, not mine), from entering your country. My problem is I have already grabbed a job in your country which pays cash in hand very well, along with hundreds of my fellow Mexican friends. I am a supervisor in a hotel with my friends who do not speak much English. I see that you are booked in here in a few months for a conference to discuss the building of this wall. We do not have any papers or citizenship and would be forced to return to our native country resulting in the closure of the hotel. As this is the only hotel around for miles, you and your entourage would have nowhere to stay. Furthermore, I and my friends have just signed a new cash in hand contract with penalty clauses and unlike politician's, our word is our bond and we intend to carry out the contract to the end.

So there lies the problem and what we need from you Mr. President is details and plans regarding the wall. For example, how long will it take to put the motion through the senate and how long for the plans to be drawn up. How long to build considering the border is nearly two thousand miles long and which end will you be starting from. One of the main concerns is how high will it be as ladders are difficult to find out here and being short arsed, means we would have difficulty carrying them. Also, should the wall be completed before we leave, will there be any guards and dogs around. I personally think the project will take longer than a year so therefore I and all my mates would like to apply for jobs building the wall. Cash in hand of course.

Yours sincerely,

Miguel Ambrosio Diaz.

28 MY HERO

Feeling very restless and tired, it had been a very difficult and traumatic last three weeks and I needed to calm down and take things easy. After putting my young family to bed early as the five of them had been very boisterous running all over the house causing mayhem leaving me with the mess. Settling down on the settee, my head on a soft cushion and slowly removing the restless thoughts out of my mind, I dozed off.

Waking much later in the early hours of a cool starry night, my nostrils twitched as a strong smell of smoke entered them. As I leapt from the settee, there was a loud crackling sound and on entering through the doorway into the next room, the place was ablaze with flames up to the roof. I was about to run into the bedroom to rescue the family when the hall ceiling fell in almost on top of me blocking my path. Choking with the dense smoke filling my lungs, I began to feel weak and went back into the lounge. The old sash window was open just enough for me to climb out onto the narrow window sill, pressing my body against the glass as it was four stories high and one slip would have been fatal. Smoke billowed out of the open window, turning away in an attempt to gulp in any available oxygen I looked down towards the street lights just as a fire engine came speeding along, lights flashing like lightening in the darkness. The firemen quickly got to work, hose pipes, ladders and turntable were assembled in minutes. I watched as slowly a fireman armed with a hosepipe and breathing apparatus, slowly rose towards me. He saw my perilous situation and delayed using the hosepipe until he rescued me to safety onto the turnstile. Glad to be there but desperate for my family to be saved, I made such a commotion which caused the fireman to risk his life.

The hosepipe was pumping water at a terrific rate onto and into the building and although the flames began to subside after a while, the density of the smoke increased. The hose was now focused onto the roof which had partly collapsed. The fireman tried to open the window but it was stuck and a crowbar was used to force it open a few more inches. He climbed in and disappeared through the smoke. Several minutes later he reappeared but his rucksack together with his oxygen tank, got stuck on the window. He removed the rucksack and threw it onto the turntable, climbed out of the window and we slowly descended to the safety of the pavement. My grief at the loss of my family was too much and I collapsed on the ground. Recovering after a few minutes, my eyes wide open, there in front of me was my three-week-old family, a bit dazed and confused but alive. The last one stepped out of the fireman's rucksack and we all happily purred away.

29 WHY ME

I know I signed the papers
They said it was a draft
I thought, lots of fun and capers
But me mates said I was daft
The danger was far too much
Afghanistan is cruel
Please send someone else
I think I have been a fool
Too late now lad, you're in the Army
The Sergeant Major said
Keep your wits about you
Or soon you will be dead
Why me, why me, I cried and cried
Don' t worry said the Sergeant
Just take it in your stride
I had done the training
That there was no doubt
But also a risk of failing
As the Sergeant bellowed out
Lift your feet up you idle sod
Your supposed to be a soldier
I softly prayed to God
I wish I had left it until I was older
Why me, why me, I cried and cried
Don't worry said the Sergeant
Think of the pride
Soon we landed in another land
It was hot, humid and dry
As soon as my feet touched the sand
I felt I wanted to cry

Who are we fighting
What's the reason, what's the cause
With bullets and bombs igniting
I stood for a thoughtful pause
Out in the desert there was an attack
Two of my mates dropped dead
From bullets and strafing flack
Whizzing past my head
Should I flee this dreadful scene
The desert, there was nowhere to hide
I thought of where I could have been
Why me, why me, I cried and cried
I held my gun and ran and ran
Through the dunes as fast as I could
I came face to face with the Taliban
And held my ground where I stood
I shot them all without fear
Just to avenge my mates
The blood poured out from my missing ear
But I avoided those pearly gates
I got sent home to recover and rest
And was confronted by my boss
You are now a true Soldier
And have been awarded the Victoria Cross

30 E BA GUM

I must look bright and smart, I have a special date
She is so very special, I must not be late
We made contact through an agency, via the internet
And share lots in common, but have never met
A bit of aftershave, as romantic as can be
I walk into the restaurant, for early evening tea
There is no sign of my mate, I feel so alone
Then a vibration alerts me to my mobile phone
I'm sorry I'm late, I'll be there very soon
Suddenly there was a glow as she walked into the room
Everything she said about herself, was so very true
I told her at that moment, I'm in love with you
In our online conversations, I told her how much I care
And had my own house and car, good teeth and blonde hair
She seemed so keen and invited me to her flat
She offered me a drink as on the sofa I sat
She cuddled up beside me and offered me some nuts
Bits got stuck in my teeth and gave me aching guts
To the bathroom I did go to ease my bitty jaws
And on return she went next for a lady's cause
Drink now blotting out my brain, my tongue I suddenly bit
From the bathroom she appeared and said, you're a lying git
In her hand she held high, my full set of false teeth
Then gave me lots of hassle and serious verbal grief
Since that day I have stayed away from dating on the line
And now I'm wed, I lay in bed and everything is fine
We kiss and cuddle, get in a muddle but there is no grief
She doesn't care I have no hair and a mug looks after my
teeth.

31 GAZUMPED AND TRUMPED

I wanted to be President of the United States
To live in the Whitehouse and entertain my mates
I haven't got a clue about being a politician
Republicans, Democrats or a Coalition
It just sounded fun and I was bored
In the polls I heavily scored.
So, on the 20th January, twenty-ten plus seven
I was sworn in and it felt like heaven
Goodbye Mr Obama and your lovely wife
Enjoy your retirement, enjoy your life
From now on things will change
Not just one or two, a complete range
For I intend to walk very tall
And around Mexico, I will build a wall
To stop the immigrants taking your jobs
Shouting their rights, voicing their gobs
Next will be China, an import tax
Stop tacky goods, it's far too lax
And there's plenty more I intend to do
To benefit Americans like you and you
Whether your rich, whether your poor
I'll improve your life more and more
In the meantime, struggle and go with your gut
I could be a while as I get my hair cut.

32 FOR RICHER FOR POORER

It was all set to be the most memorable day of their lives. Janet and Andrew had been friends since primary school, moving on to senior school then attending separate universities. As close neighbours, they never lost contact and were inseparable once their education was complete. They became engaged on Janet's twenty second birthday.

Andrew went into merchant banking while Janet became a P.A for a multi national company in the city. Their futures were looking extremely bright, they had lots of friends, wonderful families and a great social life. A couple of years later, Andrew was suffering from stress due to the high-pressure job and his general manner began to change. Instead of going home after work, he could be found in the local pub drowning his sorrows with work colleagues. Things did not improve and he began to stay out partying till late. Information came to Janet's attention that he had been seen in the company of other young ladies and this she found quite disturbing. He was confronted with it but denied all knowledge and she was doubting he could be trusted. A few months later Janet saw Andrew out with another girl, there was a big row, they stopped seeing each other. Emotionally, both suffered, Andrew realised what he was losing and sorted himself out both at work and in his mind.

Now months later they were standing at the alter, about to be married, holding hands and totally in love. The congregation of family and friends sat silent as the Vicar spoke the words, 'If anyone here present knows of any just cause or impediment why these two people may not be joined together in holy matrimony, speak now or forever hold your peace.' Just as he finished speaking and all was silent, a young woman holding a baby appeared and stood at the side of the groom. Janet was livid and slapped Andrew across the face. The Vicar quickly took control of the situation and said to the young woman, 'Do you have something to say.' She replied, 'Yes I do, sorry for the interruption but could you please speak up as we cannot hear at the back.' She quietly returned to her seat.

33 A BUM DEAL

The meal with the family was absolutely great
We went to the curry house but not too late
I had a vindaloo which was very, very hot
And soon I felt a movement in my twitchy bot

The waiter said it's mild but obviously he lied
I sat there in pain, to keep it in I tried
I burped and farted and thought this is getting close
And the pain in my gut was absolutely gross

I had to leave the table and go to the loo
For any second now a number two was due
It exploded with force, a really good blast
But I didn't care, the discomfort had passed

I reached for the paper but it was nowhere to be seen
Panic set in as I needed a clean
Should I use my shirt, vest or towel
Then a minute or two later, I let out a howl

The power went off, it was totally black
As I reached for a towel on the chrome rack
I fumbled around and pushed it up my doufa
But in the dark, I'd used the bloody loofah

34 COUNTER MEASURES

After two weeks in office as the new President of the United States, Donald J Trump managed to seriously deplete any popularity he had in the first place. New regulations for this, new regulations for that, messing with the abortion rules, oh and let's not forget the biggest one of all, the immigration bill. Trump says that Mexican drug barons and the criminal fraternity involved with them are entering the United States illegally, selling drugs and committing serious other crimes. We all know that the first item on his agenda was to propose building a high wall along the almost two thousand miles border with Mexico. He then intends to recruit five thousand security staff to ensure the border is not abused. He has already put in new regulations affecting businesses, border controls and airport security. Anyone with slightly incorrect papers or looking suspicious is being held and told they cannot fly or will be deported. This is affecting young and old who have family in other countries, creating unemployment and despair. Due to the unpopularity of these regulations and Trump himself, mass protests have been taking place in cities around the world. Furthermore, he has been urging other countries to follow Britain's road and leave the E.U to strike up an alliance with America.

After being in office for three months, Trump realised that he was becoming a hated man and decided to travel around Europe to bolster his popularity. He visited London where thousands turned out to protest against his visit and his actions. Extra police had to be drafted in, there were riots, cars set on fire, shops burned, street fighting with Trump supporters. The visit was cut short and he and his entourage left in a hurry.

A few days later he visited another major British city and once again there were protesters, not thousands but hundreds of thousands bringing the area to a virtual standstill. Music was blasting away, banners were everywhere, it looked menacing but there was no rioting, fighting or any damage caused, just a peaceful demonstration. Trump, with a wall of police in front of him, began to address the masses. Suddenly the crowd surged forward, the police cordon broken, Trump feared for his life and fled inside the hotel. This is serious said the President to his advisors, we need an urgent counter measure.

The manager of the hotel told them that the leaders of the protest would like a meeting to express the views of the crowd. Trump readily agreed as he saw an opportunity to bond and increase his status. The leaders were shown in and demanded that the intended wall with Mexico be scrapped as a lot of them were immigrants and as history shows, our city was built by immigrants and we have a strong bond with Mexicans. Trump was not amused that a bunch of banner waving yobs were trying to force his hand on such a serious subject. He asked to be given thirty minutes to discuss the issue and retired to another part of the hotel.

As he and his entourage sneaked out of the building and entered the hotel private car park, they got the shock of their lives as there were his drivers and security staff, naked except for their underpants, tied to the railings. The four black Presidential limos' lay on bricks, their wheels missing. The protest leaders said, 'sign the declaration not to build the wall and we'll give ya yer wheels back.' Trump reluctantly signed the document and said to his aides,

'That's the last time I go anywhere near Liverpool, bloody Scousers!'

As a result of actions by the people of Liverpool, the city is now twinned with the capital of Mexico.

35 SPEECHLESS

As I went to the loo for a little tinkle
I looked in the mirror and saw a dreaded wrinkle
I'll have to stop drinking this rich red wine
I'm far too young to have a line
But time passed by as parties we had
Then one day I thought, your face looks bad
Lines and wrinkles very thin lips
I need some Botox or tucks and nips
So off to a clinic to be assessed
They told me my face was really messed
A course of injections, a bucket load of filler
I looked like the star out of Thriller
But during the procedure something went wrong
and they accidently injected my tongue
mouth swelled up, I can't say a word
and my husband thinks it's totally absurd
Five thousand quid and you can't even speak
Worth every penny you crazy freak.

36 BREXIT

They couldn't make a decision, didn't know what to do
Even though highly paid, they passed it to me and you
What do we know, what do we say?
We watched the news, read the papers every day
Then we had to vote, in or out they said
And Cameron's career was very quickly dead
The remain party tried hard but Brexit prevailed
and Cameron felt that he had failed
But what about all the barmy rules made by the E U
Just to make life difficult for the likes of me and you
Don't sell bent bananas, cucumbers must be straight
Prunes are not a laxative, shit, too late
Lose your licence if you're a diabetic
Sell eggs by weight not a dozen, it's all pathetic
Jams not jam if less than sixty percent
And the Tampon tax, at least that went
Child allowance for immigrants

No wonder Westminster is full of rants
But article 50 is being given a push
Although as usual there is no rush
At least the barmy rules will disappear
And the E.U millions can stay here
We will resurrect the N.H.S
Brought to it's knees, In a total mess
And if we sign up with America on immigration
Make a point of improving that 'special relation '
Britain will be great and never again stumped
Unless of course we get well and truly 'TRUMPED.'

37 THE LEARNER DRIVER

Good morning Mr. Driving instructor, how are you today
Have you got over me driving the car down a one way
We came out safe and sound at the other end
So now I have learnt my lesson, for my test could you send
Brake, brake! you shouted, so I braked very hard
As you hit the dashboard with your yellow card
Blood was everywhere and the pain you must have felt
Was it my fault you forgot to fasten your belt?
In a bad way, a hospital you did need
So, with foot hard down I set off at speed
Past all the cars, flashing lights so bright
Speeding over junctions through the red traffic light
Get out of the way I scream and heavily blow my horn
As I hear erratic breathing, the instructor looking forlorn
A handbrake turn, a double de clutch
From a learner driver it's asking too much
A Police car right up my backend
Sorry guys I have to save my friend
Thirty miles per hour the signpost states
As we take to the air through the railway crossing gates
The Police car has gone, no siren or flashing light
As through the hospital entrance, the instructor very white
Will he live I ask the medical staff?
Of course, he will they quietly laugh
It's not his injuries that are causing the pain
But the sight of you just missing that train.

38 THE SEMI SCOUSER

In Cyprus they say I am a scouser, but they haven't got a
clue
I'm not even born and bred and my jokes are never blue
I was born in the Midlands but only till I was two
Then we moved close to Liverpool in rural pastures new
A little country village, church on the hill
No sign of a scouser, well, not until
The council built Kirkby, so very close by
I was only eight when our residents did cry
We don't want all these scousers so very close to us
They will downgrade the village and ride on our bus
But many years later Kirkby was complete
And it was inevitable that one day we would meet
Yes they had their problems, crime and poverty
It wasn't really their fault, there were no jobs you see
But when you got to know them, a surprise was in store
For as time passed, you liked them more and more
They may not have had much money, but they made up for
that
As they borrowed a cup of sugar and invited you for a chat
The warmth and kindness they offered was alien to some
And if you needed help, it was quickly done
In your time of sickness, hardship or despair
You could always guarantee, a scouser would be there.

N.B., I was brought up in the village of Melling, saw the first pipes being laid for new Kirkby in 1952.

39 A POOR RELATIONSHIP

We had been together for several years, in the beginning it was love at first sight. I could not do enough for him, all I wanted was to keep him happy, care for him, share my love and passion for the finer things in life, enjoy a good solid relationship. In return I expected him to reciprocate and show me lots of affection, be attentive, snuggle up close and be there when I need him.

At first things were cosy, we would lie on the couch watching television, A romantic comedy, his head on my lap as I caressed his lean body. Sometimes we were so happy and contented, we just fell asleep together and eventually snuggled up in bed. He had nothing to complain about, I pampered to his every whim, made his meals, let him go out at night with his mates, often till very late as I knew he would always return to me. One night he came home in the early hours making a right racket as he could not get the door open, I let him in, he just walked past me, I confronted him,
he was in a foul mood and went for me.

Things got nasty, we had a fight, he drew blood. I shouted hurtful things, told him to piss off as I didn't like him anymore, I struck out and injured him, blood was flowing fast. I panicked and rushed him to the clinic. Maybe it was time we parted, things were being taken for granted. Maybe he should find a new partner, someone who understood him more than me, I wouldn't blame him, I can be a pain in the arse at times. I was feeling very guilty for what I had done and I confessed to the doctor that I was not always a good partner, I was too clingy and needy at times. One day I loved him the next I didn't.

He said 'Madam, welcome to owning and loving a cat.'

Inspired by entertainer Melissa Williams and her cat

40 TOTALLY CONFUSED

I felt totally rejected and neglected, no one had bothered with me for days and I was feeling really miserable. My life needed spicing up, but how and when I had no idea. A week went by, still nothing and I realised I must sort things out. One day I found myself in a large room, it was lovely and warm from the heat of the electric fire, the lights were on and the radio was playing soothing music. I began to feel excited. I searched the room, hoping I could make a female connection but there was none to be found, I felt isolated. The following evening, I was back in the room, music was softly playing and there were lots of people in various states of nakedness lying on the furniture and every bit of the floor. Wine was flowing freely and there was much laughter and sexual sounds of pleasurable moaning and groaning. The totally nude female at the back of the large leather settee looked very inviting, I was extremely close, I felt a spark, a connection. Suddenly I was pushed from the rear and I swiftly entered her, I could tell immediately that she was turned on as there was a sudden surge as we bonded together. We both became overwhelmed and overpowered in the heat of the moment. It was an electrifying few minutes as her juice began to flow, I lapped up the current moments then realised any second now I was about to explode. Bang !!, I exploded, everything went black, there were murmurs and moans from the people in the room but then they just continued with their pleasures and ignored us. I found it all so erotic, I did not want to leave my new-found friend but suddenly, I was pulled off her even though I fought to remain, things got a bit heated then someone came and defused the situation. The lights, fire and radio came back on, as I was escorted out the door I looked back and asked if I could see her again, she replied, 'I am sorry, it is not possible on this occasion and I have to re-fuse.

41 CINDERELLA'S GHOST

Cinderella's mother had died and she was forced to live with her stepmother Lady Tremaine and her two older step sisters who were horrible to her and ugly. They had a cat Lucifer which had wild staring eyes and would sit on the stepmother's knee as she stroked it and she also gave a blank expression.

One evening a messenger called at the house and invited them all to a grand ball at the Kings palace. It would appear that the King wanted his son and heir to find a bride and all were invited. Cinderella knew there was little chance of her attending the ball, beautiful as she was, the evil stepmother had a passionate desire for one of her daughters to marry the young Prince. Even so, Cinderella set about finding a dress and came across one that had belonged to her mother. It was a bit old fashioned and oversized, but with the help of costume jewellery discarded by the ugly sisters, she soon had it altered and looking glamorous. When the sisters and stepmother saw Cinderella and how beautiful she looked, they flew into a rage and tore the dress from her. 'Where do you think you are going,' they screamed. The stepmother told her she would not be going to the ball and instead she was to carry out many chores which would keep her occupied all night. The three of them left for the palace, leaving Cinderella distraught and alone.

A short while later a fairy arrived and Cinderella was mesmerised. 'Who are you' she enquired. 'I am your fairy godmother,' was the reply. 'Would you like to go to the ball?' she asked. 'I would love to but I have all these chores to do,' said Cinderella. The fairy Godmother waved her magic wand and whoosh! all the chores were suddenly done. But I do not have a dress, the ugly sisters ripped it to bits,' said Cinderella. The fairy Godmother waved her wand again and Cinderella was dressed in a magnificent ball gown fit for a queen with exquisite glass slippers. Lucifer the cat was sent into the basement and after a couple of trips, came back with five live mice and two lizards. All went outside and with a swish of the wand a fabulous coach appeared with four white horses, two footmen and a coachman who held the door open as Cinderella stepped inside. 'Now don't forget,' said the fairy Godmother, you must leave the palace before the clock strikes midnight or the spell will wear off and everything will disappear, and you will return to your normal self.'

Cinderella entered the ballroom, all eyes staring at her including the Prince who quickly asked her to dance with him and they stayed together most of the night. Suddenly the clock struck midnight, Cinderella fled across the ballroom, down the grand steps but fell and lost a glass slipper. She continued through the doors only to find a pumpkin waiting for her. Her gown had been replaced by her tattered dress, the coach, horses, footmen and coachman, all gone. Fearful that she would be seen, she picked up the pumpkin and ran all the way home. She hid the pumpkin in her room as a memento of the night. The following day the ugly sisters mocked her, jealous of her association with the Prince. They piled on the pressure and gave her a serious hard time.

About a week later it was Halloween night and the sisters went to bed early as they were fearful of what might happen. In the early hours, they were woken by a strange noise and flashing lights appeared on the ceiling. As they both sat upright to investigate, fear set in as there on the dressing table was a pumpkin with a terrifying face glowing in the black of the night. They sat there unable to move with sheer fright, suddenly the pumpkin began to rise very slowly and a number of mice and two lizards could be seen desperately hanging on as it came closer to the now rigid sisters. Minutes later, it was circling round the room, narrowly missing their noses, faster and faster it went as though out of control. By now, the sisters were screaming in terror and made a run for the door, ducking as the ogre pumpkin passed overhead. The door was now mysteriously locked. The pumpkin collided with the curtains setting them on fire, the room quickly became engulfed in flames as the panic-stricken sisters tried to break it down without success.

Cinderella and her wicked stepmother, woken by all the commotion, ran to the room and tried to force the door but it was hopeless. They began choking as their lungs filled with smoke. They hurriedly began to make their way downstairs, but the wicked stepmother fell and banged her head, rendering her unconscious. Cinderella tried to help but it was no use, most of the house was on fire and she had to get out quickly. She stumbled down and out through the front door into the cool air of the night. She breathed heavily, composed herself and as she turned round, was confronted by an exquisite coach drawn by six white horses. Two footmen stood at the rear and a coachman held open the door. She stepped inside to find her Prince Charming sat there. 'Is this your slipper ', he enquired. She tried it on, 'Yes, it is,' she replied. They embraced, their love glowing. 'This is for you' he said and handed her a note. Cinderella slowly opened it with shaking hands, it read, I hope this has not been an inconvenience, I am wandering around the superstore in Fairyland looking for a new wand, this one has been playing up a bit lately. Your Fairy Godmother.

Cinderella and her Prince lived happily ever after.

42 LOVE HURTS

He only found out when he returned home from the pub. The locks had been changed and it was impossible to gain access. After trying several times, he threw his keys down in a fit of temper and began to shout and bang on the door. There was total silence, no response. His frustration heightened and he began to kick the door and bang on the windows, still nothing. 'Bitch, open the effin door or I will break it down,' still nothing. Now totally agitated and frustrated he picked up a brick and flung it with as much force as he could muster, through the front window. Neighbours came out, 'what's all the commotion,' said one. 'Oh, it's you, I might have known.' They stared at the man going berserk. 'what do you think you are doing you mad man.'

'The bitch won't let me in,' he said.

'I am not surprised,' said another, 'the lady who lived here was ninety-seven and she died this morning, you . . . you drunken bastard, live next door.'

He made a move towards the house next door but his path was blocked by the neighbours. He continued to use abusive and threatening language and people were concerned that he may hurt someone. Suddenly the sound of a police siren could be heard, the locals felt relieved as the officers got out of the car and arrested the man for his actions plus criminal damage. They struggled to contain him with his arms and legs kicking and waving about wildly. He was put into the back of the car and taken to the police station. Due to his violent past and record he was given a six months suspended prison sentence, a restraining order to stay away from his wife and home and ordered to keep the peace. A few days later he was back at the house but peacefully. 'I just want to talk,' he said. His wife was having none of it and threatened to call the Police. 'I just want to come in for a few minutes,' his voice filled with anxiety. 'You can't, my mother is staying, now go away.' Reluctantly he left full of bitter disappointment. He knew that once gain he was in the wrong due to his behaviour as a result of his heavy drinking but he had never before failed to make up with his wife. They had been married for a long time and although no children, they had always had a rock-solid partnership and were total soul mates despite his problems.

He found it strange her mother was staying, something she had never done before even when he was away working. They had fallen out years ago when his wife's father had died and left most of his estate to her. Her mother was very bitter and apart from the occasional rant fuelled by a few glasses of wine, had not spoken to her for years.

Now retired and on state and company pension, he had very little to occupy his life. His wife was his main reason for living apart from booze. Eventually he was arrested for violating his suspended prison sentence and was sent to prison where he was put in a rehabilitation centre and received help. Slowly and surely, he came off the booze. The time passed and he came out of prison, a new man full of enthusiasm to start a new beginning with the love of his life, his wife. Smartly dressed, with a bunch of roses in hand, he called at the house, his wife appeared. There had been very little contact and although slightly apprehensive he was confident that he could win her back.

'What do you want,' she asked in a defensive manner. He explained that he was now sober and a reformed character due to hospitalisation and wanted to come in and chat with her. 'Go away, my mother is staying,' she replied and shut the door. Sadly, once again, he left bitterly disappointed. Yes, there was a long-standing rift between the mother, his wife and him and yes mothers and daughters do reconcile in times of stress but theirs was too deep, something was not quite right.

On returning to his temporary accommodation, he tried to think things through. At one stage a drink flashed through his mind but so strong was his desire to have his wife back, the thought passed. It was over fifteen years since he had spoken to her mother, he decided peace of mind was required so he rang her number. He nearly put the phone down a couple of times, this was crazy.

'Hello,' said the mother, there was no mistaking the voice, he swiftly ended the call, sat down and thought, what the hell is going on. Was she telling him her mother was staying to keep him away or did she have another man in the house. He became highly mentally aroused, enough to drive anyone to drink but he had been well cared for at the rehabilitation centre and he resisted. It was a very restless night but in the morning, he was determined to get to the bottom of things.

He parked close to the house, a man appeared from inside followed by his wife, she moved close and gave him a peck on the cheek, they smiled at each other and he went on his way. So, it is true, she has got another man. His emotions were running high, this was all too much. The front door had been left open, he walked into the hall and peered into the lounge to find his wife fiercely hugging a good-looking woman. They kissed each other a few times. Out of sight he was about to burst in with more anger and resentment than he thought possible when suddenly there was the dreaded mother-in-law. Stay calm, stay calm he thought, then knocked on the lounge door and stepped in. Before he had chance to say anything, his wife threw her arms round him and hugged and kissed him passionately. 'What's going on,' he enquired, 'and why were you kissing those people.'

His wife replied, 'While you have been in rehabilitation I realised you were very serious about me and our marriage, I made friends again with my mother who has paid for a self-contained extension at the back of the house and will be moving in soon. The couple I was hugging and kissing own the company who built it and I was showing my appreciation. I hugged and kissed you because you are my husband and I love you. Welcome home darling.'

43 THE CONFESSION

Father, forgive me for I have sinned
What are your sins my son?
Well, I broke next doors window while playing football
Accidents happen my son, is that all
 Well no, not quite, I kicked their dog one dark night
You see, it crapped all over my shoe
Peed on my pants, covered me in poo
It's one of Gods creatures, you have to forgive
But I kicked it so hard, it didn't live

A strong confession off your chest
If only, you haven't heard the rest
Pray continue, I'm here to understand
Well, six months ago I robbed a shop, stole a grand
What was the reason, were you broke?
Yes, I met this girl I wanted to poke
You mean sex, how old was she
Just fifteen between you and me
Under age, that's against the law
I know, but it was too late once we were on the floor
We've been at it for months, there was just no end
Until she introduced me to her best friend
Another six months, she's like a rabbit
And now I can't get out of the habit
If she's old enough where's the sin
As long as she isn't kith and kin
But Father, there lies the problem, since I first kissed her
We fell in love, but she's my little sister.

44 AUTUMN

I am a leaf, part of a tree
There are lots of leaves, not just me
I live up high towards the sky
But in the autumn I fall and die

A golden brown I had become
As I softly landed on my bum
No longer will I sway in a gentle breeze
But on autumns ground I will freeze

Stiff and brittle, a soul now lost
As over my body sets a cold hard frost
Local children trample on me
As they search for conkers in the tree

Unaware of my final fate
They throw up sticks with a mate
I am no longer a leaf, just a broken bit
As conkers fall from being hit

But in my life I did some good
As I swayed on a branch in a wood
Some thought it useless, totally bonkers
But without me, there would not be any conkers.

45 BEST MATES

I lay there feeling relaxed, not a care in the world, no one to bother me or interrupt my peace and quiet. My mind wandered, who am I, why have I got this idyllic lifestyle. I felt like stretching but I was so laid back and relaxed, nothing moved, I just lay there. My two best mates who shared my home were much the same, we just laid around all day, every day. The home was dark and small so the three of us were very close.

One day, the home was struck by a violent force and the whole end of it was ripped away from the main structure, it was a frightening experience. One of my mates was dragged away, never to be seen again. The violent force stopped, me and my other mate just lay there, too shocked and scared to move. Daylight flooded our severely damaged home, but not for long, there was a loud bang, we felt our home move and then everything went black.

As time passed we wondered what our fate would be, we did not have to wait much longer. There was the sound of rumbling, daylight appeared, the whole home shook violently, my mate fell out leaving me all alone. More rumbling then the daylight disappeared and all was still. Time passed very slowly, months went by, nothing, just silence and darkness. I felt I was withering away, very weak and feeble due to being stuck in the same place for so long. Eventually the rumbling sound was heard, the home shook, I was dragged out, gripped by two prongs. Was I following my other two mates, but where was that, my fate was unknown but I was soon to find out. The prongs held my neck tightly as two more grabbed the other end of my body and began to pull hard in opposite directions as though stretching me. Suddenly one end was freed and my body sprung back to normality although my neck was still held tight. This happened three or four times. I then felt a projectile being pushed inside me and I was plunged into darkness inside a tunnel. Back and forth I went, battered by the sheer force of the projectile hitting the tunnel walls. For a split-second daylight appeared then all went black.

Later, I found myself severely injured, my skin torn apart and I was covered in a sticky substance. I was lying amongst tons of rotting rubble; the stench was nauseating. I looked sideways and there were my two mates lying motionless in a skip, their bodies ripped apart.

My life had been short, most of it lying around, then in a few minutes, just like my mates, I was completely destroyed. During the last seconds of my existence, I hoped that if ever I came back again, it would not be as a condom.

46 THE POWER OF A SMILE

I woke in the morning feeling depressed
But what was to happen I would never have guessed
I wandered the streets in a state of confusion
My life was a mess, I came to conclusion
No one noticed me, no one cared
Not even ' hello ', not a word was shared
Alone in a crowd, turmoil in mind
Surely there was someone who could be kind
Too busy on mobiles as forward they flee
Facebook and Twitter, no time for me
In a world of their own, where can they be
That they have no time for the likes of me
A bench I spied, so rest awhile
It was then I saw your wonderful smile
It brought me pleasure, it brought me hope
As you told me how in life I could cope
You smiled and smiled and said don't worry
Bought me tea and a nice hot curry
I may be homeless and full of despair
But you changed my life with a smile, because you care.

47 RUMOUR HAS IT

Have you heard about Daisy May?
Beds a different bloke every day
Some are rough some are tall
Some are smart some are small

Doesn't matter who they are
Along as they own a fair-sized car
In the back seat banging away
Sometimes more than one a day

The Vicar's daughter, who'd have guessed
She's out bonking while people are blessed

Black or white she doesn't care
Whether they have teeth, spots or hair
And the other thing I got told
She's not bothered if they're young or old

I told all my friends, they said, 'not Daisy May
And stood there shocked, in total dismay
Another friend said she's up the duff
But finding the father could be tough

Such a nice girl last time we spoke
Married to a Bishop, a lovely bloke
I'm not quite sure if it's all true
So I'll keep it a secret between me and you

I am not one to gossip, not one bit
But it could be true, rumour has it.

48 BLIND DATE

The newspaper ad said she wasn't half bad so
 I thought I'd give it a go
But when I got their I shuddered and stared,
 I saw she was a pro
Now I'm no prude but I thought it rude
that she should charge for it
Look at your clock, it's been round the block
and you don't look very fit.

I'll buy you a meal if you give me a feel
but that's as far as it goes
As for kissing your face in some dark place,
you will have to get rid of your nose
After a bag of chips, one or two rips,
her boobs fell to the floor
She said for a pound, I'll lay on the ground
if you want a little bit more

I fumbled around and found a pound
So she lay there on the floor
I ran to the car which wasn't very far
and swiftly opened the door
But the car wouldn't go, why I don't know,
and suddenly she was there
Pressing on glass, bearing her ass
With tits all wobbly and bare.

It was then that I saw, fingers four,
one thumb but only one leg
I said what's your name and what's your game,
she said I am called Meg
I said, your so small you can hardly crawl
and you charge a quid
With only one leg you should beg,
so I will make a bid

I'll forget your clout if you charge nowt,
now lean against the car
At it I went, like a regular gent,
she said, don't go too far
We rocked and swayed, fumbled and played,
she stood there on her one leg
Then suddenly we fell, it hurt like hell
as I landed on top of Meg.

Her wig fell off, there was a deep cough
and I could see she had some stubble
I thought, what the hell as I heard the bell
 I think I am in trouble
I jumped in the car, drove very far
and thought I must be mad
So since that day, I have stayed away
from page seven with the personal ad.

49 THE GRASS IS ALWAYS GREENER.

Teresa Green could not really afford to do the euro millions lottery, her husband Richard had been out of work for fifteen years and had health problems. Their financial state was really dire and slowly getting worse day by day. Their two children, Kate fourteen and Paul, thirteen were always demanding money for clothes and school plus social events, although Paul did help with his paper round. Teresa's part time job in a local store kept food on the table but the bills were becoming a lost cause. They had already gone through the process of debt management which had given them some respite for a while but eventually even that became engulfed in misery as she totally lost control.

Her job entailed selling lottery tickets and each week she would read about all the big winners and how it changed their lives. She knew the odds of winning were crazy but people were winning every week, why not her she thought. She was so much in debt the lack of a couple of pounds spent on the lottery would not make much difference to her situation. She began buying two tickets a week leaving them at work as she did not want her husband complaining of wasting money. The weeks and months went by, nothing, not even a tenner. Despite the odds, like millions of other people, she would sit and dream of a jackpot win of millions. It brought some inspiration and hope into her life. No more worry, no debts or people threatening to take her to court. A huge luxurious home in large grounds in the country, swimming pool, sauna, a massive garage full of prestige cars, fabulous exotic holidays with the family. A gardener, cleaner and able to help out friends. Oh what a fabulous life it would be.

The desire to win became an obsession and she began to spend more and more, then one day, bang! it happened, she did it, she won. Mind running out of control, all the dreams came flooding back, her body was tingling with the excitement of it all. The big house and all the trappings had become so much closer. If only. If only she craved, if only I had got those last two numbers!

A week later after paying some debts out of her winnings of one hundred and two pounds, she closed the door on her small rented house for the last time and reluctantly handed the keys to the bailiffs.

50 FECKIN CORN

I am a nuisance, I am a corn
I sit with my owner watching porn
And when he wants a nice cool beer
The look in his eyes is serious fear

He tries to stand but remembers me
Then falls to the floor on one knee
'Bastard,' he shouts as I drive him insane
I find it amazing he remembers my name

He scratches my head, picks at my nose
Wishing I was anywhere, except his toes
He takes me for a walk, he has no choice
But all I hear is the yell of his voice

Feckin corn he screams in pain
And scratches my head once again
A plaster he says will do the trick
With fumbling hands, he makes it stick

Does it bother little ole me
As I cause him to fall on one knee
I am a corn, I am the boss
As for your pain, I don't give a toss

The plaster's warm, a cosy home
Even though I'm all alone
So take the problem in your stride
Hobble with me side by side.

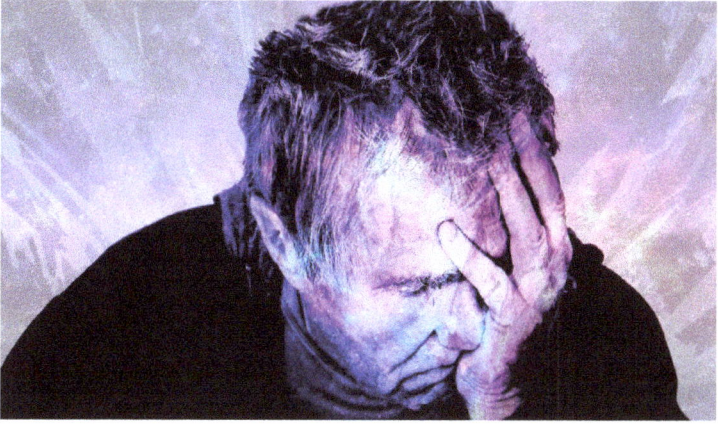

51 QUEST FOR LOVE, PASSION AND FREEDOM

I had been thinking about it for a long time, nearly a year, ever since I decided that I was totally in love and my mind and body had been enraptured in the sheer beauty. I was out of control and had difficulty stabilising my conscience and thoughts. Never in my life had I ever thought that I would be considering leaving everything behind, my life, my wife and two children, my friends, my job as a medical practitioner and all that I owned. I was not happy with my life and saw this bonded fixation as an escape into a world of love, passion and freedom. I could easily give my mind body and soul, for if everything worked out the result would be overwhelming and we would be together for the rest of our lives, in love and totally happy.

We first came into contact through the internet and slowly we got to know more about each other as time passed. The more I found out the more I wanted us to be together. Maybe I should not have continued the relationship for so long and tried to make a go of things in my life but that became an impossibility. I had loved one for many years but now it was time to move on and love another. Finally, all exploded at home, I packed my bags and began a long and lonely journey into the unknown to fulfil my dreams.

I booked a passage on a boat, not exactly a cruise ship as I did not have a lot of money. It was a bit cramped and the facilities were far from five star but if it got me to the love of my life then that is all that mattered. It was a long and hazardous journey with twenty-foot-high waves tossing the boat around, there were times when I thought we were not going to make it and people were screaming in total panic. After several days, the sea having subsided, we reached the mainland with much relief. I was directed to my accommodation, a bit basic but I was only staying for a short while before moving on to the next stage of my journey. Unfortunately, transport was difficult to find and I remained there for several weeks, the electric and water was cut off and food was in short supply, this resulted in the toilets not working properly so hygiene was of a serious substandard. Eventually I managed to board a bus leftover from the second world war and we steadily made progress in the searing heat towards my final destination. Unfortunately, the bus broke down after several days and I was forced to walk a rough and desolate route with my small rucksack containing a small amount of food and drink. I had to stay out of sight as I had no passport or official papers to legally be in any of the countries I was attempting to travel through. My food and water ran out, I fell to my knees in sheer exhaustion, my body dripping in sweat, mouth dry and desperate for liquid with the fear of starvation running through my brain now lacking in oxygen.

I woke up in a hospital bed, where, I had no idea. A drip was slowly flowing into my arm, I felt so weak and helpless. It was at this point I began to think that I must be mad chasing a dream driven by emotions of love and passion, like a lot of people I should be at home with my family but the belief and powerful feelings I had were too strong and I knew I had to carry on.

A week later I had regained some strength. After being interrogated by the immigration authorities I was told that I would be returned to my hometown. Despair and anger set in, they were right to do this as I had no right to be there but I had not travelled a great distance under cruel circumstances and close to death to give up now. In the early hours of the morning I silently crept out of the window and disappeared into the warm darkness, free to continue my hazardous journey. I had no idea in which direction I should go so after distancing myself from the hospital I sat down out of sight and waited for daylight to appear. Birds tweeted as the sun rose quickly, the town came into view, the high street was void of life apart from a couple of stray cats. After a short while I came across a bicycle and peddled as fast as I could eventually arriving at a train station were I hid in a goods train boxcar. It soon moved off, where it was going I had no idea. I woke several hours later and found myself in a dockyard full of containers, cranes and most important of all, ships. I made some enquiries and to my jubilation found one leaving in a couple of hours for my final destination. The officer in charge had no hesitation in allowing me to work my passage and several days later I arrived. I was given a lift in a shared car and as it sped through the beautiful green countryside on a warm summers day I saw the love of my life, the one passion that had kept me going. The embrace was very emotional, I lay on top face down in the buttercup strewn field, I had finally managed to enter the dream of my life, I burst into tears as I cried 'I love you England, I love you.' Now to set about bringing my lovely family over here from Syria.

52 MIXED EMOTIONS

After the break up of a five year on and off relationship, thirty-eight-year-old Tim Meeham decided that he would like to settle down and get married. His job as a sales representative for a top brand drinks company had taken him all over the world, often resulting in ill feeling causing friction between him and his partner. A three-month stint in Asia was the final straw before his partner decided enough is enough and left.

Tim gave up the travelling and took an office position in an attempt to keep her happy, but it was too late, things had got to a point of no return. He had friends, male and female, but there was no romantic link.

As he sat on the busy London underground train heading towards the office in the city, Tim gave his position in life some thought and concluded that he must go out more and meet people and make new friends, that way surely romance would come into his life.

'Tickets please,'Tim barely looked up as he thrust his ticket upwards towards the inspector. A few months later with no romance forthcoming, Tim went for an after work drink with some colleagues in the bar close to his office, it was busy, very busy as they edged their way to the bar.

She looked stunning and stood out from the crowd, Tim's eyes sparkled as his gaze became transfixed on her bright deep brown eyes, a smile of innocence played with the excited thoughts in his brain as he swiftly flickered his eyes over her figure hugging short dress, taking in the perfectly shaped legs before returning to her face and exquisite short hairstyle. Never had he seen his ex partner looking so beautiful.

After months of dating and socialising, she moved back in with him and they decided to get married. Tim's brain was awash with mixed emotions, he loved her but the love was not the same as he had been searching for, the love that takes over your brain and your life and leads you to being out of control, hence the phrase, "hopelessly in love." The desire to settle down and get married was strong and despite his concerns a date was set for the wedding in four weeks time.

Tim heard, 'tickets please' in a soft voice. He raised his eyes, what he had been searching for was there, hand outstretched. He pushed the ticket forward, gently caressing her smooth fingers, she responded doing the same, it was only a second or two but it sent Tim's heart into overdrive. Her uniform and cap seemed to enhance the moment. She returned the ticket, her eyes glazed as if to say, I seriously fancy you. She moved on as the train came to a halt and Tim left to go to work.

Over the next couple of weeks he could think of nothing else, he was supposed to be organising the wedding but his troubled mind although filled with joy, refused to function in that direction as it was heavily engrossed elsewhere. He began to have doubts about his relationship with his partner and wondered if he was doing the right thing by getting married. A few days later he thought, this is crazy as he hardly knew the girl on the train, not even her name, his mind said, sort things out, get motivated as the wedding was drawing closer.

A couple of days later he returned to the bar with his colleagues. In a soft-spoken voice the girl of his dreams, the ticket inspector, introduced herself with a wonderful smile. He was totally mesmerised and spent most of the evening chatting to her and gently holding her hand. His life was being turned upside down, all he could see and hear was her. He fought his emotions fiercely and set about the wedding plans. The day finally arrived, a few friends and work colleagues attended at the small quaint church in the village. His bride to be looked stunning as they waited at the alter for the clergyman to commence proceedings. As the final words were said, I now pronounce you man and wife, his bride whispered, 'what has been your most memorable moment?'. Tim replied, 'Tickets please.'

53 THE WRITER'S DILEMMA

Why do I write, I don't know
I pick up a pen and watch it flow
What it writes, what it says
Baffles me for days and days
I get the urge and rack my brain
And hope I won't go totally insane
It's just the mind playing games
Like a spark that bursts into flames
But the flames so quick, the brain can't cope
So I scribble away fast and just hope
The idea blossoms as I move down the page
But I have no ending and feel the rage
The character comes then the plot
But still the ending I have not got
What if the brain decides to rest,
I'll never complete this story quest
Then suddenly, like a flash in a pan
I'm scribbling away as fast as I can
It all comes together, the scene is complete
Until the next time, I'll put up my feet.

ABOUT THE AUTHOR

Richard Palmer was born in Stafford U.K on 6th May 1944. The second eldest of four brothers, he lived in Melling, Lancashire, a rural village a mile from Aintree Racecourse, Liverpool, until aged eighteen. He was educated at Maghull Secondary Modern School and Bootle Municipal Technical College, Merseyside. He served for eleven years in the Police Force and many years in the motor trade. His writing capabilities began at an early age with short stories, poems and newspaper articles.

His first book, "RICH INSPIRATIONS," Promiscuous Poems and Twisted Tales was very successful on Amazon and in Cyprus.

After the death of his wife Barbara, aged forty-six, in 1991, he became a member of Liverpool Writers Club and produced a collection of poems. Years later, Rich and new wife Linda ran 'Firkin House', their B & B in Hoylake, Wirral, U.K, before retiring to Paphos, Cyprus in 2012. There he is secretary of Paphos Writers Group and past co. Editor of 'The Main Sheet' newsletter at Paphos International Sailing Club.

Further information can be found on the short story and poem pages on his website,

www.thefirkinwebsite.com

www.ingramcontent.com/pod-product-compliance
Lightning Source LLC
Chambersburg PA
CBHW060039040426
42331CB00032B/1296